Hi-Fidelity Marriage

J. ALLAN PETERSEN

‖‖‖‖‖‖‖‖‖‖‖‖‖‖‖‖‖‖‖‖‖‖
Y0-CZP-517

POCKET GUIDES
Tyndale House Publishers, Inc.
Wheaton, Illinois

Hi-Fidelity Marriage is adapted from *The Myth of the Greener Grass* by
J. Allan Petersen, copyright 1983 by J. Allan Petersen.

Library of Congress Catalog Card Number 85-52234
ISBN 0-8423-1396-6
Copyright 1986 by J. Allan Petersen
All rights reserved
Printed in the United States of America

97 96 95 94
7   6   5   4   3

CONTENTS

The Truth about Infidelity

Infidelity within marriage is not a new idea. It is not a product of the so-called sex revolution or of the New Morality. Extramarital affairs have been with us for thousands of years.

"When the Pharaohs ruled Egypt," New York psychiatrist Alexander Wolf points out, "the husband's virtue, continence, and marital faithfulness were required of him, and his infidelity was dealt with harshly."[1]

Sexual promiscuity has always been considered a negative influence on the family and society. Even *Playboy* magazine, hardly committed to strong marriages, discovered in a carefully selected survey that the *overwhelming majority* of both men and women were against extramarital sex for people in general and for themselves in particular.[2]

However, a call for fidelity in the eighties is like a solitary voice crying in today's sexual wilderness. What was once labeled adultery and carried a stigma of guilt and embarrassment now is an affair—a nice-sounding, almost inviting word wrapped in mystery, fascination, and excitement. A relationship, not sin.

WHAT PEOPLE THINK ABOUT AFFAIRS

Of the 100,000 women respondents to the *Redbook* survey of 1974, 30 of each 100—almost one-third—had had affairs with other men. And if a woman had experienced premarital sex, she was much more likely to have an affair. Twenty-six of the thirty had engaged in premarital intercourse.

Among wives thirty-five to thirty-nine years old, 38 percent had been unfaithful. For wage-earning wives, the percentage jumped to 47 percent—almost half.

According to *Redbook,* nonreligious wives are twice as likely as strongly religious wives to have sex with men other than their husbands.

All of this, in spite of another survey that showed that 86 percent of those questioned believe extramarital sex is always or almost always wrong. Another 11 percent feel that special circumstances must be considered. Fewer than 3 percent say infidelity is not wrong at all. What we say we believe and how we live are sometimes poles apart.

SEX—IT SELLS

Sex, sex, sex. Our culture is near the point of total saturation. Books, magazines, billboards, movies shout it ceaselessly. TV, the most powerful and immediate medium, trumpets it in living color. Every day, all day, the messages bombard us like pellets from a brainwashing gun: "Get all the sex there is. All kinds. Anytime. Don't miss out."

The Louis Harris-conducted study in 1978-79 polled 1,990 men between the ages of eighteen and forty-nine and concluded that "the increased emphasis men are placing on self-fulfillment, pleasure, and doing one's own thing is dramatically altering America's traditional value system. The emerging self-oriented values represent a new personal liberalism. It is not a form of the old social liberalism."[3]

Translate this philosophy to marriage and it says, "Fidelity is out; affairs are in." If your marriage does not provide at all times all you've ever expected, dreamed, or fantasized, and fails to bring you the constant sensory pleasure and fulfillment you deserve, find it elsewhere, enjoy some "healthy adultery."

WHAT'S WRONG WITH AN AFFAIR?

Though extramarital sex is more glamorized and more available than ever, are the results as positive as the promotion? We used to talk of the guilt, the pain, the assassination of self-esteem, and the self-deceit of cheating. Have these disappeared with the kerosene lamp and can life now be one big sexual orgy with no problems, no regrets, no reverberations?

Medical doctors Alexander Lowen and Robert J. Levin chorus a resounding NO:

> There are at least three ways in which infidelity can be disastrous to the future of any marriage.
>
> *First, it inevitably causes pain to the other.* A marriage exists when a man and woman are bound together not by law but by love, and are openly pledged to accept responsibility for each other, fortified by the feeling of total commitment that extends from the present into the future. Virtually all such marriages begin with faith—which is to say that when a man and a woman entrust themselves to each other, they do so believing that neither would ever try to hurt the other, that each will contribute to the other's happiness, and that together they will seek fulfillment.
>
> The first breaking of that faith . . . happens when one partner decides to turn away from his mate in search of intimacy or fulfillment—and keeps the decision a secret. This is the true betrayal of trust. A man cannot or will not talk to his wife about matters that concern him deeply—and then discusses these concerns with another woman whose company he enjoys. He must keep the relationship secret, because it would wound his wife to know the truth—and this, in turn, reinforces their separation.
>
> *Second, infidelity masks the real problem.* To whatever extent infidelity temporarily eases the superficial symptoms of discontent in a

husband or wife—such as feeling unattractive or unappreciated—it camouflages the real malady and permits it to grow worse. Instead of seeking an honest confrontation, with all its risks and promises, both accept the dishonesty of infidelity—in most cases, one actively, the other passively. Distressed by the thought of a separation or divorce, they pretend to be faithful while they search for satisfaction outside marriage.

Third, it is destructive of the self. The unfaithful partner who pretends that by keeping his affairs a secret he protects his wife and safeguards his marriage practices the deepest deception of all: self-deceit.

The person who does not care strongly about anything or anyone can, by tailoring his idea of love to suit his needs, tell both wife and mistress that he loves them—and believe it. The lies are unconscious, and therefore, not marked by pain. This is the ultimate act of self-deception. Instead of resolving conflict, it perpetuates it; the deluded person lives a lie. He is sick and does not feel the fever.[4]

So, there is pain, affecting everyone involved. There is something destructive about an affair—destroying one's inner integrity, a partner's self-esteem, and the possibility of intimacy, and it reverberates through future generations, affecting children and grandchildren. The law of the harvest remains inexorable. "Don't delude yourself into thinking God can be cheated: where a man sows, there he reaps."[5]

Eight Facts about Affairs

1. No one is immune to an extramarital affair.
2. Anyone, regardless of how many victories he has won, can fall disastrously.
3. The act of infidelity is the result of uncontrolled desires, thoughts, and fantasies.
4. Your body is your servant or it becomes your master.
5. A Christian who falls will excuse, rationalize, and conceal, the same as anyone else.
6. Sin can be enjoyable but it can never be successfully covered.
7. One night of passion can spark years of family pain.
8. Failure is neither fatal nor final.

CHAPTER 1

Could an Affair Happen to You?

Things don't just happen. Every action has a cause. Actions do not arise spontaneously from a vacuum. There are contributing factors, pressuring forces, and personal reasons beneath the surface.

Marriage failure is the same way. When a partner is involved in an affair—a one-night stand or a long-term relationship—there are reasons. *The affair is a sign of a need for help—an attempt to compensate for deficiencies in the relationship, a warning that someone is suffering.*

Causes of marital infidelity vary as much as the personalities involved, but I believe they can all be considered under one of four general headings: emotional immaturity, unresolved conflicts, unmet needs, or unfulfilled expectations.

A SELF-QUIZ
Respond to the following statements to determine whether or not an affair could happen to you.

	Yes	No
1. Sometimes I wish I could be dating many different people again.	_____	_____
2. I often feel unacceptable to my spouse.	_____	_____
3. When I was a child, I usually received whatever I wanted from my parents.	_____	_____
4. I feel independent of God and most other people.	_____	_____
5. My spouse and I often disagree about the amount of time he/she spends on his/her job.	_____	_____
6. My spouse and I often disagree about how we spend our money.	_____	_____
7. My spouse and I often disagree about how to raise our children.	_____	_____
8. I would love my spouse more if he/she were just a little different.	_____	_____

EMOTIONAL IMMATURITY
Adolescence is often a traumatic time. This period was not intended to be permanent but is usually a bridge from the dependency of childhood to the interdependency of the adult. These transition years are often marked by immaturity, rebellion, fickleness, self-doubt, and experimentation.

9. I can't remember the last time my spouse complimented me on the way I looked or on something I had done. ____ ____

10. Sometimes I think I married the wrong person. ____ ____

11. I wish my spouse and I had a more active sexual relationship. ____ ____

12. My spouse and I don't have much time to do things together anymore. ____ ____

13. I believe marriages are made in heaven. ____ ____

14. The right marriage can make a person happy. ____ ____

15. Having children is a good way to hold a straying spouse. ____ ____

All of the above statements have been cited as contributors to extramarital affairs. If you answered yes to any statement, you, too, are vulnerable.

_____

Unfortunately, some people in their forties or fifties are still adolescent in their behavior. Instead of marriage being our last best chance to grow up, according to Joseph Barth, it becomes a reflector of our perpetual immaturities.

Consider my friend Joe. Married three years—two children. During his dating years he liked to think of himself as God's gift to the girls and went from one partner to another. Forced into marriage by his girlfriend's unexpected pregnancy, he wanted to be faithful but still had a roving eye. According to him, his wife was all a wife could be. But in his mind he was still the unattached, flirtatious teenager.

Parental indulgence can prepare a child for perpetual immaturity and marital infidelity. Permissive parents, fearful of thwarting their children's desires, give them everything they ever cry for. The children are never denied, never taught the necessity or value of discipline. The adolescent who has had every whim immediately indulged will not become a marriage partner of strength and unselfishness. The man growing up without hearing and respecting the word NO will not take it as an answer when he is being tempted to satisfy his wants and desires.

Pride also sets up a man or woman for a fall. As Solomon says in the Bible, "Proud men end in shame, but the meek become wise."[6] An emotionally mature person has a realistic sense of his own human weakness and the need for dependence upon God and other people. He does not parade his strength and flex his muscles before God and others.

A well-known evangelist became lifted up with pride. His work was prospering, radio and TV programs thriving, invitations to speak increasing. He began to manipulate people to his selfish ends. As he became

14

more brazen, he traveled alone with his secretary. When someone asked him about this, he bragged, "I can handle it. Don't worry about me. And even if I decide to divorce my wife for this girl—no big deal. People will forget about it in a few months."

Of course, he fell—like a bird shot from the sky, and his marriage and ministry fell around him.

In short, *each person determines the extent of his own emotional immaturity. Affairs do not arise out of bad marriages; they are developed by immature people.*

Five Signs of Maturity

1. I trust God.
2. I accept my own imperfections.
3. I am committed to lifelong learning and growth.
4. I keep my future ahead of me, forgetting the past.
5. I seek to understand and do God's good will.

UNRESOLVED CONFLICTS

Conflicts in life are inevitable. In the intimacy and constant togetherness of marriage they are unavoidable. Children, money, sex, stress, in-laws—you name it. The young couple walking down the aisle with stars in their eyes, believing in a happily-ever-after, is in for a rude jolt.

Each person has his own set of idiosyncrasies brought over from childhood and experience. He feels comfortable with them. Contemplating marriage, he's looking for someone who will also feel comfortable with him as he is and, at the same time, meet his emotional needs. This is usually someone quite different from himself, and that's part of the attraction. Now combine these two sets of temperaments, personalities, and individual characteristics, and there's bound to be friction.

A stalemate develops. One partner insists on his way. The other matches with the same determination and continues to agitate. Neither one has love strong enough to cover the other's weaknesses and focus on the other's strengths. The point of conflict then enters into the reason given for straying.

Ten Common Causes of Conflict in Marriage

1. "The job is everything."
2. "Our whole life is a money struggle."
3. "My mother-in-law isn't bossy—she's tyrannical."
4. "We disagreed about our daughter."
5. "An audience with a queen."
6. "A terrible housekeeper."
7. "A conservative background."
8. "The criticism just wore me out."
9. "Maybe it's just the mid-life blues."
10. "Super-clean Jean."

Conflict over work. The American man sees less of his family than any other husband and father in the world, noted Pearl Buck. The home wreckers are often the job, the corporation, the career. But no amount of business success can make up for failure at home.

I still grieve over Harold and Phyllis, the young couple I met and counseled in Washington. He was a workaholic—first one at the office, last one to leave. And, of course, it paid off handsomely. His salary, commissions, and promotions increased. Then came a new home, new car, new clothes, fine restaurants. Their one child, Brad, was growing up in good surroundings but with little father interest.

Phyllis began to feel increasingly ignored. "Doesn't he realize we don't need more money, more things? We need him," she complained.

The boy joined Little League. Harold just couldn't squeeze out time to attend the games. But he made arrangements: "Phyllis, be sure Brad has a way to the game and a ride back home." And when the son returned home he couldn't even tell his father about their victory; Harold wasn't there. When he finally did get home, the boy was asleep.

Every week, same story. Loneliness and resentment increased, driving mother and son to turn against the father.

"An affair with another man never entered my mind," Phyllis recounted. "This friendly guy was at all the games and took special note of Brad and me since we were always alone. One thing led to another, as they say."

Harold's wife became another man's mistress because Harold had a mistress: his job.

Conflict over money. "It was money that drove me into the arms of another man—at least, the conflict and pressure of money," complained Arlene.

Conflicts over money are customary in marriage. The income, expenses, credit, and debts, coupled with the different meanings money has to each spouse, can make for a stressful, volatile situation. When a man loses his job and can't support his family, he often feels his masculinity threatened. And in those circumstances, some men think that making a sexual conquest will help reconfirm their manhood.

But let's return to Arlene. "We had a chance to buy this house and it was a great bargain. But we had to furnish it, and just the basic things put us head over heels in debt. Then Bill had a car accident and there were a lot of things connected with it our insurance didn't cover.

"I tried getting a job to help out, but by the time I'd paid the baby-sitter, bought clothes, and paid for my lunches and all that, I was making less than ten dollars a week.

"Our whole life is a money struggle. Every month it's a frantic shuffle to see what bills we can pay and what we'll have to put off. I get the nice job of calling creditors to tell them we can only pay half of what we owe this month. The constant worry, the embarrassment—you can just imagine what it's like.

"And then one day I ran into Dave, who was in my class in high school. He took me to lunch in a really fine, fancy restaurant. Oh, the relief! The sheer pleasure of getting to talk about ordinary, everyday things and not once hear him mention money.

"The guilt I feel about my affair is like little drops of acid eating away at the back of my mind. But I have to have some escape, some release from this constant financial worry and tension."

Conflict over children. "What do you see as the basic problem in your marriage that relates to your present infidelity? Your marriage always seemed strong, and you and your wife compatible." This was my question to a businessman in California when he asked for help in extricating himself from his extramarital affair.

"My wife and I had a serious disagreement over one of our children," he answered immediately. "It became a wall between us.

"Our daughter was beginning to date and neither one of us really knew what to do. My wife was fearful that she would come home pregnant very soon, considering some of the crowd she was running with. So she said, 'Forbid her to go out with them. We must protect her; it's for her own good.' I was concerned too, but wanted to approach it differently. I wanted to tell her we trusted her and put her on her honor. We discussed the merits of each approach until there was no more to say. But we kept on talking. Not talking, really, anymore. We were arguing, criticizing, lashing out.

"Naturally, our daughter played this to the hilt. She knew that if we were fighting each other she'd be off the hook. She sided with me and against her mother. Feeling rejected, my wife accused me of being weak and vacillating—and maybe I was. The blow came, as far as I'm concerned, when she said she had lost all respect for me. I was devastated. The problem had shifted from the girl to our marriage.

"I walked about like a zombie. What had been a great marriage seemed now to be a hollow shell. I wasn't looking for an affair—I've always been faithful—but I was looking for a little comfort, a boost, a prop for my sagging spirit, I guess. This other woman provided that."

Disagreement doesn't hurt a marriage, but criticism kills it. We can strongly disagree on many matters, respect each other's views, work it through, and still love each other. But when the disagreement turns to criticism of the other person, no one can take that very long. Attacking the person instead of working on the problem is a sure way to suggest to your partner that he or she might have made a mistake in marrying you. And he might look elsewhere to remedy that mistake.

UNMET NEEDS

"My partner doesn't understand my needs." Every husband and wife has felt this way at some time though he or she may never have verbalized it audibly. When needs are not met, the door is opened for infidelity—someone else to meet those needs.

Marriage is a need-meeting relationship. It was so during the courtship and continues till the last day a couple is together. No one is so unselfish or altruistic that he marries with a pure desire to meet someone else's need and ask nothing for himself. And wanting our needs to be met is neither selfish nor sinful. It has been said that *love is the accurate estimate and supply of another's needs.*

The essence of the marriage promise is "I will meet those needs." The wedding vows say it:

- "To have and to hold"—commitment
- "For better or for worse"—belonging
- "For richer, for poorer"—loyalty
- "In sickness and health"—support
- "To love and to cherish"—faithfulness
- "Till death do us part"—companionship

That is a tall order. No wonder we all sometimes fall. I'm not suggesting we dilute the vows, but rather that we understand how they're translated and applied to our partner's everyday needs.

We have five basic needs that a marriage partner can meet.

Attention. Sara wrote me after our counseling sessions, "It's going to be hard for me to give up the love I had for someone else and to say no to the first person who really listened to me. For thirteen years with Bruce I have felt so unloved and unwanted. He never notices my cooking, the way I look, how I try to keep the house for him. He never pays attention to me. He takes me for granted and I really don't think I'm important to him."

One guilty straying husband said, "I'd come to feel like no more than a piece of furniture. I was nobody around my own home, nobody worth noticing, listening to, or loving. This is what I mean," he said. "I came home one night some weeks ago and my wife was putting the baby to bed. I started to kiss her but she turned up her cheek and talked about the baby's rash. Did you ever try to kiss someone with a safety pin in her mouth? Why couldn't she look at me? Talk to me? I'm the guy she married."

Acceptance. Every person has a deep-seated need to be accepted for his or her own individual value. It is our job to love our partners, God's job to change them. Author John Drescher quotes counselor Ira J. Tanner, "Any attempt to move one's mate in an effort to match them to our fantasies is arrogance on our part and an insult to them. It divides, breeds anger, and causes even greater loneliness."[7] And, I might add, it pushes the mate into other, more accepting, arms.

Ruth and Jack were personal friends of Evelyn's and mine—in fact, neighbors. But her affair brought them to me for counsel. "He wanted me to be Mother Theresa, Betty Crocker, and Cheryl Ladd rolled into one," Ruth said. He was determined to squeeze me into his mold. Nothing I could do pleased him anymore.

"Adultery was the farthest thing from my mind. I wasn't looking for sex—even though that had deteriorated in our marriage, too. I wasn't looking for an affair to get revenge, make my husband pay, or even get his attention. I was just beat. That was all. And when another man noticed me, smiled a few times, talked pleasantly, and liked me the way I was—that was it. I was a dead pigeon."

Affection. Many partners cheat in marriage for nothing more at the start than a desire for a little affection. The things that put the glow in the days of courtship and early marriage—touching, holding, hugging, kissing—cannot be stashed away now in the closet with all the old wedding announcements.

"We haven't touched each other for over two years, at least not intentionally." These were the words of a pastor's wife who had come to one of our seminars.

Her voice beginning to crack, she continued, "I've not been much of an affectionate type, not that I don't enjoy it, but my husband and I've had to work so hard to keep our churches going. Always overloaded, always exhausted.

"When my husband evidenced no desire to show affection or any need for it, I assumed he was just that kind and those things didn't interest him. So I didn't push it either, and kind of stayed out of his way."

"How did your husband get involved with this other woman?" I ventured.

"Well, she offered to do some volunteer work in the church office. We wondered, a time or two, if we should keep her, since she dressed in such an obviously sensual way. But my husband felt that since she was a new Christian he could help her. I felt she'd be no temptation to him since he was not interested in affection." By now she was sobbing.

"Then what happened?"

"How blind I was, oh, how blind! She would make a special point to be in his office for every little excuse. She kidded him, touched him playfully, and, well, something came alive in him, I guess. He became a different man. That's when he told me he didn't love me anymore and was going to leave the ministry and move in with her."

Admiration. Mark Twain said, "I can live for two months on a good compliment." For every negative comment a parent makes to a child, he must give four positive comments to keep a balance. So in marriage. Verbal praise nourishes the relationship.

According to my friend Dr. Ed Wheat, "A wife's sense of her own beauty depends greatly on what her husband thinks of her. She must be nourished emotionally with praise and never diminished by criticism."[8]

Famous author Marabel Morgan asks, "What motivates the man to be responsible and to succeed in his ambitions? What one incentive will help a man remain stable, faithful and loving to his wife and family? Admiration can put back the skip in a husband's walk, a sparkle in his eyes and the flutter in his heart. He will dare to dream again and believe in his abilities because you've told him you do."[9]

What to Admire in a Man

His role as a husband and father.
His appearance and manner of dress.
His mental capacities.
His dependability on the job.
His masculine strength.
His athletic ability and coordination.
His sense of humor.
His courage.
His tenderness and sexual capacities.[10]

What to Admire in a Woman

Her role as a wife and mother.
Her appearance and manner of dress.
Her mental capacities.
Her diligence in the home or on the job.
Her physical fitness.
Her creativity.
Her sense of humor.
Her kindness and generosity.
Her tenderness and sexual capacities.[11]

Activities. Many marriages crash on the rocks of infidelity because they become dull. Boredom sets in. The routine becomes a rut. Go to work, come home, watch TV, go to bed—week after monotonous week.

"We don't do anything together anymore," is a common wifely complaint. "No dates together without the kids, no recreation, no concerts, no shared interests or projects, no fun."

Great or potentially great marriages all suffer if neglected. Read again Benjamin Franklin's familiar verse: "A little neglect may breed great mischief; for want of a nail the shoe was lost; for want of a shoe the horse was lost; for want of a horse the rider was lost, being overtaken and slain by an enemy—all for want of little care about a horseshoe nail."

No one person can meet all of another person's needs. Some needs are met by others, some by our vocations, some by God alone. To expect one's partner to provide what only God can provide will affect every other area of our marriage relationship.

But just as no person can take God's place, God does not take the partner's place. We have been created to fill needs for each other that only another person can fill.

UNFULFILLED EXPECTATIONS
Most of the things that most of us believed when we entered marriage are not true. These myths and legends have been passed through many generations, and though everyone's experience denies them, we still hold to them as tenaciously as a drowning man to an unconnected rope. I've talked with second-and-third-time divorcees who still be-

lieve and hope these myths will prove true for them the next time around.

Believing these legends creates conscious and unconscious expectations in people that doom their marriage from the start and set it up for infidelity. They become disappointed, weakened, and vulnerable.

Let's consider three of the dangerous myths.

"Made in Heaven." This trademark on any marriage means what the expensive manufacturer's label means on a pair of jeans: quality. No flaws, no rips, the finest material, hand stitching, designer styling. As one company says, the quality goes in before the name goes on.

So if our marriage is made in heaven, if God brings us together, it is bound to prosper. That didn't work in the first marriage and it hasn't worked since. No one would question that God brought Adam and Eve together, but that didn't assure family success.

This legend gives false comfort and security. "God made us for each other" implies that our personalities dovetail—our temperaments are complementary. We are ill-prepared for the shocks of disagreement and conflict, times when everything hits the fan—the stalemate—the impasse—the blowout.

This myth becomes an excuse. When romantic love fades, its flame flickers. The old snap is gone, our partner doesn't perform the

27

same, and deterioration sets in. Then comes the cop-out: "I guess God didn't really bring us together in the first place."

I've heard this scores of times, and I always answer: "I do not know whether or not your marriage was made in heaven but I do know that all the maintenance work is done on earth."

"Marriage Will Make Me Happy." One reason marriage gets bad press is that it isn't the cure-all it is supposed to be. And no people in the world make greater demands on marriage than Americans. We still believe marriage is our great hope. It will separate us from our past, give us all the love we need now, and assure us of a contented old age. "Happily ever after" is still in our dreams.

One divorced husband told a friend what many would not have the courage to say: "God bless my dear wife; she tried so hard. She just didn't have it in her. She simply did not know how to make me happy."

His parents had tried and failed. Others failed. So he took a wife and gave her a shot at it. And she failed. But he'll try again, I'm sure, and give someone else the privilege!

This myth also promises a false escape. "My mother didn't like me; my dad didn't lace my shoes right once; we lived on the wrong side of town; my schoolteacher failed me. Marriage will be a haven where I can drop anchor. All the past will be forgotten. It will be a new beginning."

It will be a new relationship all right, but the past will trail you like a bloodhound. Your past will affect your marriage more than your marriage will alter your past.

This legend creates dependency. If I believe my partner will provide what I need, I become an emotional cripple. The quality of my life is determined by others. I live through them and make them morally obligated to provide my well-being. When they fail to produce what I think I need, they are blamed for my failure. I have given them the power to destroy me.

It says, happiness is a result—love is a feeling. Both of these concepts encourage a marriage partner to be passive—to wait, to react, to see which way the ball bounces.

But the truth is that happiness is a choice. Abraham Lincoln often said, "Most people are about as happy as they choose to be." You cannot choose your *feelings* of happiness, but you can choose the *actions* that will bring those feelings. That's why Erich Fromm said, "Love is not a victim of my emotions but a servant of my will." The Bible says the same, "Let us *practice* loving."[12] Love is something you do.

"Children Are the Glue." There's a common belief that children hold a marriage together. A companion fable says, "Our marriage may not be too strong, but the presence of children will bring a unifying focal point. If we both focus on rearing children, our own differences will go away." That's like adding a match to a powder keg and sitting on the cover.

This myth makes a false promise. Children

don't solve marriage problems; they aggravate them. They're very poor marriage counselors. Every study of marital satisfaction shows there is a decrease when children are born. By the time the third child arrives, marital satisfaction has taken a nosedive.

This should not surprise us. What does a child bring to a marriage? The inescapable presence of a dependent, demanding, selfish, vulnerable creature with two ends to wipe. Certainly this is going to change the schedule, encourage frustrations, exhaust the mother, and decrease the bank balance. It will bring out the best and worst in us.

The primary focus must be on marriage, not on the children. We must concentrate on what we give to children, not on what they bring to us. Marriage is permanent, parenting temporary.

These three marriage myths have one feature in common, one underlying fallacy: that you can get off the hook. That someone else—God, partner, child—is responsible for your well-being. That someone else will be the initiator.

This sets you up beautifully for an affair. If God didn't bring you the right partner, and your partner and children don't bring you happiness, why not look elsewhere? Somewhere you'll find it.

And that's a myth, too.

Test Your Temptation Quotient

When you were born you were married—married to a companion who will walk the road of life with you until the end. You will never awaken any morning or retire any night without this companion's being right at your side.

This companion will never leave you for reasons of nonsupport. You can never sue for separate maintenance. It is impossible to get a divorce. Whether you like it or not, you and this partner will be together until death do you part. Temptation—your lifelong companion.

Everyone is tempted. Temptation knows no strangers. No one can evade it or avoid it. It is an inescapable fact of life.

In fact, if a person thinks mistakenly that he is safe from temptation, he is already vulnerable.

A REALISTIC LOOK AT TEMPTATION

Its author. "Never, when you have been tempted, say, 'God sent the temptation'; God cannot be tempted to do anything wrong, and he does not tempt anybody."[13] During the enticement of temptation, it is easy to rationalize and make God its author. No, the Bible says, God does not send the temptation. To do so would be totally contrary to his nature, his objectives, and his Word.

Who tempted Adam and Eve in the Garden of Eden? Who tempted Jesus for forty days in the wilderness? Satan, the devil, is called the tempter, the old serpent, and our great enemy. "He prowls around like a hungry, roaring lion, looking for some victim to tear apart."[14] And he has a tremendous success pattern—having succeeded to some degree with every member of the human race.

Its nature. Mark this well: temptation is not sin. It could never be. The Bible says Jesus "was in all points tempted like as we are, yet without sin."[15]

Our reaction, our response, determines whether or not we sin. In fact, temptation all by itself is about the weakest thing in the world. All alone it is utterly powerless. To succeed, temptation always needs a partner—someone to agree with it, to dance with it, to open the door for it, to welcome it in.

When a girl approached me in a hotel lobby and smilingly asked, "Would you like to have a little fun tonight?" it was only a temptation. An enticement to infidelity is not sin. Our hospitality makes the difference.

Its objectives. Sin is the objective of temptation. However seemingly innocent any temptation appears to be, the devil's sole purpose is to get you to sin. Not just to impede your progress a bit, to put a few hurdles in your path, but to nurse you along as a midwife and help you give birth—to sin.

The devil's objective is not to have a world full of drunkards, prostitutes, and acid heads. These are not good advertisements for him. But sin, on whatever social level, with whatever sophistication, thwarts God's wonderful plan for your life, and to this sinister and destructive end the devil is forever totally committed.

HOW TEMPTATION WORKS

Temptation appeals to your human desires. Your God-created needs. And these are not evil. The appeal of temptation is always to satisfy a legitimate need in a wrong way or at a wrong time. The inner desire itself is good, to want it satisfied is fine, but how and when it is done makes the difference. The good or evil is in the way these needs are met.

Desires for friends, love, praise, success, acceptance, intimacy—these are all good. To satisfy these by dishonesty, manipulation, selfishness, and violations of God's truth leads us to sin.

Exactly so with sex. Every person is a sexual being, with sexual desires, sexual attractions, and sexual feelings. All of this is God's idea. Nothing is or ever could be wrong with sex. Because sexuality is God's gift, there can be no fault, flaw, or evil in it. But man has a history of prostituting God's gifts and using them to his selfish advantage and detriment.

Temptation appeals to the weakest place in your life. Everyone has a special weakness. As a cunning strategist the devil marshals his strongest forces at the weakest place in the line. Our differences in temperament, personality, inherited weaknesses cause us to respond uniquely to different kinds of temptation.

Sex is a bigger problem for some people than others. They are more highly sexed—their emotional needs are greater. Temptation to an extramarital affair may pose a greater battle for them than for the more conservative type.

STEPS TO A FALL

1. Temptation begins in the mind. The most important sex organ is the mind. An affair starts in the mind long before it ends up in bed. The clandestine relationship began as an innocent thought in the secret recesses of someone's mind. Thought is the source of action. The body is the servant of the mind. Thoughts determine character. Our character is cast in the mold of our concentration.

The communists have learned through their brainwashing success that if they can convert and control the thoughts of people, they can reform their character and enslave them. They believe, as Emerson said, "The key to every man is his thought." Thoughts

34

rule the world. Good thoughts never produce bad results nor evil thoughts, good results.

Napoleon Hill crystallized what I think is the most important and staggering concept concerning the mind. "The only thing any person has complete, unchallenged control over is his thought—his state of mind."

You have no control of your circumstances or your nature; you can't control heredity or environment; you can't control your physical makeup or mental capacity, other people, friends, or enemies—the past or the future. There is only one thing you can control: you have the power to shape your thoughts and fit them to any pattern of your choice.

2. Thoughts become fantasies. Thought of evil or evil thought? What is the difference between them? Suppose I read a legitimate book or magazine, or watch a wholesome TV show. Something I see—an ad, a paragraph, a picture—causes a thought of evil to flash into my mind. Is that sin? No. I drive down the street and what I see on a billboard or hear on the radio causes a suggestion of evil to invade my mind. Is that sin? No.

Or I meet a woman who is bright, charming, vibrant. Though not flirtatious, she has a radiant personality. A thought flits through my mind that this girl is a beauty, well-endowed, and I know she is sexually attractive to any red-blooded man. Anything wrong with that? No! It is not sin to hear the hundreds of transient and tempting suggestions that knock on my mind's door every day and all life long.

But when that passing thought of evil is welcomed, given hospitality, mulled over and over with the consent of your will, it becomes an evil thought. If I open the door, warmly invite this stranger in, give him an easy chair to relax in, and encourage additional conversation, the stranger has become my friend. This friend now helps me construct a picture—simple at first but ultimately with details and in living color—of all that this friendship can mean to me and the needs that will be met by it.

That picture is a fantasy and fantasies are previews to the desired action. An affair is experienced many times in fantasy before the time and place of the first rendezvous are set.

3. *Fantasies create emotions.* At this point, the subconscious part of the mind does not differentiate good from evil and only reacts to the suggestions and pictures given to it audibly or in the imagination. The suggestions come from the self-talk that we all practice, often not realizing its tremendous power and influence.

Everyone engages in self-talk, unconsciously reacting to every situation, analyzing, judging, reliving, expressing our beliefs, our fears, our desires. Psychologist Dr. David Stoop has made a study of self-talk and notes, "We usually speak out loud at the rate of 150 to 200 words per minute. Some research suggests that we talk privately to ourselves in our thoughts at the rate of approximately 1300 words per minute."[16]

As the fantasy regarding the possibility of

an affair develops, our minds affirm and enhance it by what we say to ourselves and the images created. "That would be fun . . . I need that . . . life has been boring . . . she's something else . . . stolen apples are sweeter . . . I don't mean anything wrong." And so on, at 1300 words per minute. Hundreds of pictures feeding the fantasy. If we repeat any of this audibly to ourselves, that autosuggestion etches the image deeper, and our subconscious mind will work to bring it to pass.

So our minds feed the fantasies, the fantasies create the appropriate emotions, and the emotions scream for the actual experiences. This is why when one is emotionally committed to an affair, all the truth and logic in the world don't seem to faze him. In a contest between emotion and truth, emotion usually wins.

A SELF-QUIZ
Respond to the following statements to measure your readiness to cope with temptation.

	True	False
1. I could never be tempted to be unfaithful.	___	___
2. I'm familiar with what the Bible says about affairs.	___	___
3. I would give anything to escape a struggle with temptation.	___	___
4. I believe it's OK to fantasize about having an affair as long as you don't follow through.	___	___

5. I haven't given much thought
   to how I would respond to an
   easy opportunity to have
   extramarital sex.   _____ _____
6. I'm often grateful for my
   spouse.   _____ _____
7. I'm committed to obeying
   God in every area of my life. _____ _____

Answers: (1) F, (2) T, (3) F, (4) F, (5) F, (6) T, (7) T.

If your answers correspond to those above, congratulations! You probably have a good grip on handling temptation. If one or more of your answers differs from those above, read the following section carefully.

SEVEN STRATEGIES AGAINST TEMPTATION

1. Deflate it by expecting it. A great part of temptation's power is in its surprising strategy. A surprise attack is an enemy's most successful tactic. How often I've heard it from sincere people, "I never dreamed I'd be tempted to be unfaithful; I thought I was safe, that it couldn't happen to me."

Since God tells us plainly that we shall always be tempted, then why not expect it? We often play a passive, defensive game instead of an intelligent, aggressive one.

A dear friend called me, and I could tell by his voice he was troubled. I didn't think much about it for I knew him to be a very strong Christian. Arriving at my office he told of a young divorcee who was destitute and how he had bought her groceries, gotten her car fixed, and tried to help her as a Christian friend. Part of her response was to become infatuated with him and invite him over for a quiet, intimate evening. "I found it difficult to say no," he said. "I was surprised that there was a struggle. I guess I thought I wouldn't have those temptations anymore."

2. Develop a biblical conscience. In a struggle with temptation we usually live our values, not our beliefs. If our conscience has been trained by the Bible and we are committed to its principles, we meet temptation with confidence instead of fear. God's warnings are the love-words of a parent telling his child not to run in the street, not to jump off the bridge, not to play with matches. They are loving protections, not arbitrary prohibitions.

3. Defuse it by not fearing it. A fatalistic fear of temptation strengthens its power over us. Some would give anything if temptation could be eliminated and they could live without a struggle. "The greatest of all temptations is the one to be without any," says Henry Drummond. Napoleon declared, "He who fears being conquered is sure of defeat."

Temptation is a chance to develop virtue and mastery—a stepping-stone to building Christian character. The man who has the most temptations has the most chance of growing in grace. Limp, fragile tomato vines can be grown in the controlled atmosphere of a hothouse. But it takes winds and storms to grow oak trees. It depends on what you want to be.

4. Decide irrevocably if you want victory. The word "victory" implies a battle. Temptation

God's Advice on Affairs

The lips of another man's wife may be as sweet as honey and her kisses as smooth as olive oil, but when it is all over, she leaves you nothing but bitterness and pain.

Drink from your own well, my son—be faithful and true to your wife. Let your manhood be a blessing; rejoice in the wife of your youth. Let her charms and tender embrace satisfy you. Let her love alone fill you with delight.

Can a man hold fire against his chest and not be burned? Can he walk on hot coals and not blister his feet? So it is with the man who commits adultery with another's wife. He shall not go unpunished for this sin.... But the man who commits adultery is an utter fool, for he destroys his own soul.[17]

is the battlefield. Indecision in a battle spells defeat. Your overall life purpose will determine how you meet daily temptations. If you waver here, you will vacillate when the pressure is on.

E. Stanley Jones states it graphically, "If you don't make up your mind, then your unmade mind will unmake you. Here is the place where there must be no dallying. For any dallying will be the Trojan horse that will get on the inside and open the gates to the enemy. God can do anything for the man who has made up his mind; he can do little or nothing for the double-minded."[18]

5. Determine your response ahead of time. You cannot wait until you are nose-to-nose with temptation to decide your response. It's too late then. In the backseat of the car, at the sales convention, on the road, at the party, together in the office—these are not the places to weigh, analyze, and decide regarding an affair. There's too much emotion. The decision is made ahead of time and only confirmed at the time of temptation.

A salesman friend was attending a dealers' convention in New York City. On a free evening he was waiting for a car with others to see some of the city's sights. But he got into the wrong car. These salesmen were not headed for the tourist attractions but for a famous swinging bar. Before my friend knew his mistake, they were on the way with no turning back. Upon entering the bar, each man was immediately joined by a girl who took him by the arm and led him to a table. His girl was saucy, pert, and dressed seductively.

"As the evening continued, the temptation was like a steam roller," he told me later. "This girl was luscious. I had all I could do to keep from grabbing her impulsively and taking her to one of the back rooms. But the thing that held me and protected me—the only thing—was that before I had left home, I had told my wife that I was hers alone, and that regardless of any enticements, we belonged to each other." His decision ahead of time saved him.

6. Discipline your mind with counteraction. It is not enough to resist the negative—we must major on the positive. No man can long keep out evil who does not keep in good.

Counteraction is the key. "Fix your thoughts on what is true and good and right. Think about things that are pure and lovely, and dwell on the fine, good things in others. Think about all you can praise God for and be glad about."[19] "Fix your thoughts" . . . "think" . . . "think" . . . "think." This is not shifting your mind out of gear and hoping some excellent thoughts drop in. Shift your car into neutral and it coasts downhill, out of control. Daydreaming is dangerous, one of the costliest disaster areas of life. We must deliberately, determinedly concentrate on what is pure, praiseworthy, positive, and honorable.

7. Discover the secret of victory. Jesus was tempted in all the same ways we are, and he overcame. He met temptation as a man, using the same resources that are available to us. If he had resorted to his divine power as the Son of God, he could have worked a miracle to destroy his enemy and to provide his needs. Instead, as a human being with all the emotions, pressures, and weaknesses of man, he met the tempter at every point.

For forty days in the wilderness, He was exposed to Satan's entire arsenal of temptation. The temptations came at the weakest point during the most crucial time. When

Christ was famished from lack of food, the temptation was to provide bread—to satisfy the need, the hunger. When Christ was feeling forsaken, the temptation was to test God's love and see if he still cared. When Christ was overwhelmed by a sense of powerlessness, the temptation was to compromise, to gain power and dominion. At every point, Christ resisted firmly, decisively.

What was the secret of his success? He was obedient to his Father. Before the temptation, he had surrendered to the complete will of God. This was the underlying principle of his life—a calm, repeated choosing to obey at each advancing step.

Obedience to a God-planned program for life is never easy, but it is the price of freedom and fullness.

How to Affair-Proof
Your Marriage

On a trip to Alaska, Evelyn and I were provided a one-week, expense-paid vacation in the fabulous Mt. McKinley National Park. We were flown into the park by small plane over deep mountain chasms and beautiful lakes and between magnificent peaks. Breathtaking scenery! We transferred to a sight-seeing bus for the five-hour trip back through mountains to the remote Camp Denali.

Like kids on their first trip to Disneyland, we were all oh's and ah's and eyes. It was a photographer's paradise. Grizzlies, caribou, moose, dall sheep, rare birds—we saw them all.

But on this forever memorable journey there were many ordinary signs along the road—warning signs: Beware of Falling Rock. Do Not Leave the Road. Camping at Your Own Risk. Also helpful signs: Scenic Rest Stops. Scientific Station. Historical Monuments.

Marriage is like that—a long and memorable journey. And it becomes more meaningful when you pay close attention to the signs. And more safe—safe from an extramarital affair.

Here are eight signs that will guard any marriage and keep you on the offensive.

DON'T COMPARE THE INCOMPARABLE

No two marriages are in any way alike. Therefore, to compare them is a negative exercise, breeding negative results. You only confirm your conviction that you have a second-class marriage—or increase your fear that you will fail in a first-class one. Both of these attitudes kill personal initiative which is necessary to a successful marriage.

Your marriage is unique—therefore incomparable. You do not compare a Volkswagen with a Cadillac even though both of them are automobiles and both of them can take you where you want to go. Everything about these cars is different even though both of them have the same essential parts and operate on the same basic principle.

The personalities and temperaments of the partners, the inherited characteristics, the opportunities, training, and experience—these all differ widely with each couple. Comparing your marriage with anyone else's can never be valid.

Also, your partner is unique. You don't need a new partner. Between you, you have the assets for building a great relationship if you are both really committed to working at it. No one else has the same potential you

Your Marriage:
A Diamond Mine

There once lived an ancient Persian by the name of Ali Hafed. He owned a very large farm, orchards, grain fields, gardens. He had many investments and was wealthy and contented. One day he was visited by an ancient Buddhist priest, a wise man of sorts. They sat by the fire and the priest recounted the detailed history of creation. He concluded by saying diamonds were the most rare and valuable gems created, "congealed drops of sunlight," and if Ali had diamonds he could get anything he wanted for himself and his family.

Ali Hafed began to dream about diamonds—about how much they were worth. He became a very poor man. He had not lost anything but he was poor because he was disconcerted and discontented because he feared he was poor. He said, "I want a mine of diamonds," and he lay awake nights.

One morning he decided to sell his farm and all he had and travel the world in search of diamonds. He collected his

have—the special combination of strengths and sweetness that God has given you. All the elements for satisfying marriage are already there if you will use them.

money, left his family in the care of neighbors, and began his search. He traveled Palestine and Europe extensively and found nothing. At last, after his money was all spent and he was in rags, wretchedness, and poverty, he stood on the shore at Barcelona, Spain. A great tidal wave came rolling in, and the poor, discouraged, suffering, dying man could not resist the awful temptation to cast himself into that incoming tide. He sank, never to rise again.

The man who purchased Ali Hafed's farm led his camel to his garden brook to drink one day. As the camel put its nose into the shallow water, this new owner noticed a curious flash of light from a stone in the white sands of the stream. As he stirred up the sands with his fingers he found scores of the most beautiful gems: diamonds. This was the discovery of the most magnificent diamond mine in the history of mankind—the Golconda. The largest crown jewel diamonds in the world have come from that mine.[20] Your marriage diamonds are in your own backyard. Don't overlook them. Don't minimize them. Mine them.

DON'T SET YOUR OWN TRAPS

Many affairs are the result of falling into your own self-made and self-baited traps. We naively grease our own slide and unconsciously do the things that set us up for a fall.

Consider your friends. In a society where flirtation is the norm and an affair is accepted behavior, you must choose and cultivate friends carefully. Friends who treat marital infidelity lightly or tell suggestive jokes and stories are really enemies of your marriage. Avoid them.

Protect yourself on the job. It is no secret that many affairs are spawned in the office and that sexual favors often influence contracts and affect promotions. One attractive and very competent secretary told me how she protected herself. "I turned down all invitations for private luncheons with men in our office—and there were many of them—because I knew myself and I knew it would be difficult not to respond to the admiration of other men. I valued my marriage too much to expose myself to those risks."

Avoid entertainment that lowers inhibitions. Take TV soaps, for instance. It is impossible to build a great marriage and be a devotee of soap operas. Their distorted drama of romance, sexuality, infidelity, affairs, and abortions encourages comparisons, dissatisfaction. Unconsciously you begin wondering why your spouse is not like "John's other wife" or "Mary's secret husband." Such fictional comparisons are bound to result in a feeling that you're being cheated in your present marriage and that an affair would bring release from your boredom.

Create boundaries. Margaret Hess has some practical suggestions.

Draw boundaries in relationships with the opposite sex. A psychologist says he avoids scheduling a woman for his last appointment. A minister keeps a counselee on the other side of a desk and keeps the drapes open. A doctor calls a nurse into the room when he must examine a woman patient. A boss and secretary can avoid going to dinner as a twosome or working evenings alone. A homemaker can avoid tempting situations with neighbors when her husband is out of town.[21]

Dr. Carlfred B. Broderick sums it up in another way. "If you find yourself in a situation involving delicious privacy with an attractive member of the opposite sex, you should begin to look for ways to restructure the situation."[22] If you do not, your foot will be caught in your own net.

REFUSE TO RELIVE THE PAST

Sawdust cannot be resawn. The old cud cannot be re-chewed endlessly. The past is now history and cannot be relived. You can do nothing about past behavior but learn from it. You can only live in the present moment; any reminders from yourself or others of the mistakes of the past will only victimize you and render you incapable of acting now. Refuse to let your marriage today be hurt by what used to be.

Each marriage partner must make a strong commitment to protect the other from crippling memories. "I will never bring up the past again. We must never let anything behind us control the future of our marriage. I will never drag any skeleton out of the closet to remind you of a past mistake, nor hold anything over you to victimize you and continue the hurt we have both suffered. The best days of our marriage are ahead of us and we will move into them and embrace them together." Remember, yesterday ended last night.

LOOK THROUGH YOUR PARTNER'S GLASSES

Because of the many temperamental and emotional differences of men and women, it is natural that they will judge their marriage differently. You cannot assume that because your needs are met, your spouse's are too.

Tom and Jan are special friends of mine in Texas. As we sat around the kitchen table recently, they told me their experience. They had just gone to bed one night. Tom had kind of spread out lying on his back while they were recounting the experiences of the day. With hands behind his head he exclaimed with great satisfaction, "I am supremely happy. We have a great marriage and family, I'm doing well in business, we're in a wonderful church. I don't know how I could be more content."

While he was basking in this euphoria of contentment, he realized Jan was very quiet, then the bed began to shake. Muffled sobs came from the other side of the bed and Jan broke out weeping. Tom was shocked, then got the surprise of his life when she cried, "How can you say that? I have never been so unhappy and disappointed. Nothing is going right. Everything is a mess."

Couples often unconsciously feel that to discuss marriage needs openly will create a strain and magnify problems.

But the opposite is true. While we assume everything is lovely, if we do not know where the fault lines are, an earthquake can be brewing and could blow everything to kingdom come.

We must know the strengths and weaknesses of our partnership. We must know how our spouse feels about the quality of the marriage. The secrets must be shared while we are able to face them positively together.

Talking to Your Spouse

Use the following questions as a springboard for discussion with your partner.
1. How do you really feel about our marriage?
2. Where do you see areas of strength in our relationship?
3. Are your needs being met—socially, emotionally, spiritually, sexually?

KEEP YOUR HANDS EMPTY,
BUT THE BOX FULL

Dr. Willard Beecher tells how most people come to marriage believing it is a box full of goodies from which we extract all we need to make us happy. We can take from it as much as we want and it somehow mysteriously remains full. And even when the box does get empty and the marriage collapses in a heap, we have not learned our lesson. We still look for a second partner that will bring another bottomless box with him so we can empty it.[23]

But marriage is an empty box. There's nothing in it. Marriage was never intended to do anything for anybody. People are expected to do something for marriage. If you do not put into the box more than you take out, it becomes empty. Romance, consideration, generosity aren't in marriage, they are in people, and people put them into the marriage box. When the box gets empty we become vulnerable to an affair.

There is a quaint little Pennsylvania Dutch restaurant in a nearby suburb where Evelyn and I like to eat. There's nothing like it in the entire Chicagoland area. The food is superb—deliciously flavored, enticingly prepared, served in large portions. When we have house guests this is the first place we think of taking them. And they always rave about it and remember it.

There is no fancy decor; in fact, it is quite plain with crowded seating and oilcloth on the tables. No reservations are taken, so we usually have to wait.

Not once have the owners cornered us and made us promise that we would return. Not once have they chained us to the tables to make sure we wouldn't leave them. Not once have they cried and whined, "How can we live without you?" And they have no discount prices. They just keep their box appetizingly full and their generous hands empty.

To say it another way, open the cage but keep the quality birdseed in the feeder.

BECOME THE HOST, NOT THE GUEST

Children should not be allowed to get married. A child fills a passive/receptive role. He expects to be served. Everything is done for him. He feels no sense of responsibility or initiative. He's treated as a guest. Children do not know how to be hosts.

No marriage can accommodate two guests—not even one guest. A satisfying marriage must have two hosts, each one personally committed to the active/initiative role of the mature adult, not the passive/receptive role of the spoiled child.

The host initiates and builds friendships. Generally, when guests are invited for a meal or social evening, they are friends of the host. Total strangers or enemies are not usually on your guest list. One of the objectives of the hospitality is to develop new friendships and deepen old ones.

Each partner in marriage should desire to say, "My spouse is my best friend." At a recent party, a Christian leader and his wife were celebrating their twenty-fifth wedding anniversary. I asked them the outstanding characteristic of their marriage. The wife answered immediately, "We have become very good friends." That is significant. You can have a compatible sex relationship and not be close friends. You can be partners in your parenting responsibilities and not enjoy an intimacy and openness as friends. You can fill your biblically prescribed roles and not accept each other as equals, which is the basis of real friendship.

What Makes a Friend?

In a survey of more than 40,000 Americans conducted by *Psychology Today* these qualities were most valued in a friend:
1. The ability to keep confidences.
2. Loyalty.
3. Warmth.
4. Affection.

The host is a careful planner. Accomplished hosts/hostesses do not get that way by accident. They plan their events down to the last detail. Nothing is taken for granted. The party that comes off so smoothly and efficiently is really the result of much thought, time, and expense.

Marriages without that same kind of careful effort and thoughtful planning will decay. The most destructive notion that marriage partners have about marriage is that it will somehow roll along on its own momentum. However, the natural tendency is to drift apart, not to grow together. Uncultivated ground grows weeds, not flowers.

Good things do not just happen. A love note in the lunchbox or under the pillow does not appear by magic. For a candlelight dinner someone has to make the reservations. Love must be planned.

The host considerately meets needs. He takes responsibility for the comfort of his guests. Music creates a relaxing atmosphere, comfortable seating is provided, appetizers and hors d'oeuvres are served. Finally, a full course meal is provided. The host makes sure the room temperature is right. Conversation is initiated and strangers are introduced so that all the guests feel at ease. He is committed to meeting their social needs.

Get a firm picture in your mind of yourself as the host and your spouse as the guest. Do you see it? You—attentive, caring, considerate, generous, an initiator. Now, how would you meet your spouse's *emotional needs?* Would you be able to carve out some quality time together? To talk about your mutual interests? To share each other's goals and dreams?

What about *sexual needs?* How would you go about meeting your partner's sexual needs if you were the host? Would you be more sensitive? More generous? More creative? Less excusing and blaming? Would you not learn all you could about your partner's sexual nature? Would you remain in ignorance? The spouse who refuses to be the host and provide for his or her partner's sexual satisfaction is just begging for someone else to stand in and meet the need.

Spiritual needs? If you assumed responsibility for your partner's spiritual development, would you become more familiar with the Bible? More aware of how to pray together and encourage one another?

ACTIVATE LOVE BY YOUR ACTIONS
Love is a skill. Love involves giving. Love is something you do.

This takes the mystery and the myth out of it—the cheap sentimentality and the irrationality. Love is an art that is learned and a discipline that is practiced. The attention and effort that go into mastering any art, skill, or vocation must be committed to learning to love. This involves discipline, concentration, patience, and commitment.

Since love actions are a matter of choice, they are not dependent on our feelings. In fact, they may be contrary to our feelings. Just yesterday a wife told me, "I no longer have any feeling for my husband. I cannot touch him and I don't want him to touch me. And you want me to reach out to him when I feel this way?" Exactly! The repeated positive action can have a positive effect on your feelings.

START YOUR OWN AFFAIR AT HOME
What are the elements in an affair that make it attractive? What does it offer? What are its unspoken secrets and mysteries? What are the qualities you can build into your marriage that will give you the feelings an affair pro-

vides without the deception, destruction, and guilt that an affair inevitably produces?

The most descriptive thing I've read about what necessities a marriage must offer to counter-attack the appeal of an affair comes from Dr. Tom McGinnis, a counseling psychologist. It is quoted by Nicki McWhirter of Knight-Ridder News Service.

Married people seek out or succumb to affairs when they feel devalued and less than fully alive. They are bored. Overburdened. It amounts to being very lonely, and it can happen in a household full of kids and babbling spouse in which there is a back-breaking schedule of "fun" things to do.

People who have affairs have the child's deep longing to be touched, caressed, held, hugged and kissed, whether they can admit it or not. They want happy surprises. That might mean a sentimental, unexpected gift every once in a while. More important, it is the dependable gift of time and caring, the present of shared ideas, experiences, stories, nonsense, and games, including sexual games. They want the world to butt out.

They want a loving friend, a pal who isn't judgmental. They want someone to convince them they're still loved, lovable, and very special. For a little while, now and then, they want out from under the grown-up responsibilities that have become predictable, dreary and difficult.

There are at least seventeen separate thoughts, qualities, characteristics mentioned here. I have isolated each of these important ideas and posed three questions about each one in the marriage test that follows. Go over these questions carefully. Consider them thoughtfully. Answer them honestly. Your honest answers can forecast a new beginning—can be a change-point. They will indicate where you can begin to change the climate of your marriage and create the situations that will give you and your partner the good feelings you need.

A Marriage Test for Wives and Husbands

A MARRIAGE TEST FOR WIVES

	Never	Occasionally	Frequently
Unappreciated I consider my husband a person of worth and listen with eye contact and focused attention.	_____	_____	_____
I take my husband for granted and forget to notice and praise him.	_____	_____	_____
I support my husband in times of failure with reassurance and affirmation.	_____	_____	_____
Lifeless I encourage my husband to think and feel young.	_____	_____	_____
I plan things we can do together that encourage romance.	_____	_____	_____

	Never	Occasionally	Frequently

I resist creative changes that could add spice and variety to our lives.

Bored
I consider my marriage a dreary routine.

I have growing expectations, plans, and goals for our marriage.

I encourage my husband to develop his talents, hobbies, qualities, and gifts.

Overburdened
I am critical of my husband because of financial problems and differences.

I support my husband in his job (in or out of the home) and encourage his success.

I do not allow my parents to interfere or create tension in our marriage.

Lonely
I try to understand my husband's loneliness and encourage him to express it.

	Never	Occasionally	Frequently

I openly express my own feelings to my husband and tell him what I need.

    _____ _____ _____

I am learning to open up and overcome the tendency to retreat into my shell.

    _____ _____ _____

Children
I let my husband and the children know that he is first in my affection.

    _____ _____ _____

I encourage a marriage-centered, not child-centered, home.

    _____ _____ _____

I give leadership to the spiritual training of our children through Bible reading and prayer.

    _____ _____ _____

Schedule
I am highly organized for each day, allowing no time for spontaneity and surprises.

    _____ _____ _____

I am a slave to the urgent request of outsiders, becoming a means to their ends.

    _____ _____ _____

	Never	Occasionally	Frequently

My expectations of my husband and children cause them to feel pressured, inadequate, unable to please.

_____   _____   _____

Touching
I find ways each day to touch and hold my husband so he knows I appreciate him.

_____   _____   _____

I enjoy the delight of caressing and hugging without insisting it culminate in sex relations.

_____   _____   _____

I keep myself inviting so my husband is not repulsed by offensive attitudes, appearance, and odors.

_____   _____   _____

Surprises
I think of special or unusual things I could do for or with my husband.

_____   _____   _____

I arrange for surprise events—eating out, entertainment, trips, weekends away.

_____   _____   _____

I think of long-term ways to stretch my husband's interests and opportunities for growth.

_____   _____   _____

	Never	Occasionally	Frequently

Gifts

I give my husband one large gift on his birthday, anniversary, and Christmas and this satisfies him all year. _____ _____ _____

I give small gifts on many unexpected occasions because I think of him often. _____ _____ _____

I usually give utilitarian gifts rather than personal ones that say to my husband, "You are specially appreciated." _____ _____ _____

Shared Ideas

I have outgrown my husband and do not positively encourage his development. _____ _____ _____

I plan relaxing times together so we can share our dreams. _____ _____ _____

I discuss fully with my husband our plans for our marriage, our children, our future. _____ _____ _____

Laughter

I do everything I can to make our house a fun place to come home to. _____ _____ _____

	Never	Occasionally	Frequently
I encourage meal times to be special, happy times with a positive atmosphere of interaction.	____	____	____
I freely share jokes and funny stories on myself rather than on other family members.	____	____	____

Sexual Games

	Never	Occasionally	Frequently
I flirt with my husband and encourage this kind of romance and aliveness.	____	____	____
I take an active part in our sex life with genuine pleasure and abandon.	____	____	____
I am aggressive in loving my husband, seeking to delight him in every way possible and not using sex against him as a weapon, tool, or reward.	____	____	____

Loving Friend

I keep my husband's confidences and do not withhold from him any secrets that affect our marriage.	____	____	____

	Never	Occasionally	Frequently

I am loyal to my husband and support and praise him publicly. ____ ____ ____

I encourage him in the face of difficulties or defeat and stand by him faithfully. ____ ____ ____

Acceptance
I have fully accepted my husband with all his personal traits and idiosyncracies. ____ ____ ____

I have forgiven everything in his past and do not hold anything against him. ____ ____ ____

I enjoy my husband and feel free to open my heart to him. ____ ____ ____

Loved—Special
I have a growing desire for my husband's happiness and comfort. ____ ____ ____

I am committed to learning my husband's unique love language and practicing it. ____ ____ ____

I constantly tell my husband how special he is as a friend, partner, and lover. ____ ____ ____

Dreariness

	Never	Occasionally	Frequently
I nag about household chores and feel tied down and resentful.	___	___	___
I resent my husband's taking time for recreation, hobbies, shopping, Bible study group.	___	___	___
I tend to be a workaholic and feel guilty about planning special days or weekends for relaxing together.	___	___	___

A MARRIAGE TEST FOR HUSBANDS

Unappreciated

	Never	Occasionally	Frequently
I consider my wife a person of worth and listen with eye contact and focused attention.	___	___	___
I take my wife for granted and forget to notice and praise her.	___	___	___
I support my wife in times of failure with reassurance and affirmation.	___	___	___

	Never	Occasionally	Frequently

Lifeless

I encourage my wife to think and feel young.
____ ____ ____

I plan things we can do together that encourage romance.
____ ____ ____

I resist creative changes that could add spice and variety to our lives.
____ ____ ____

Bored

I consider my marriage a dreary routine.
____ ____ ____

I have growing expectations, plans, and goals for our marriage.
____ ____ ____

I encourage my wife to develop her talents, hobbies, qualities, and gifts.
____ ____ ____

Overburdened

I am critical of my wife because of financial problems and differences.
____ ____ ____

I support my wife in her job (in or out of the home) and encourage her success.
____ ____ ____

I do not allow my parents to interfere or create tension in our marriage.
____ ____ ____

	Never	Occasionally	Frequently

Lonely

I try to understand my wife's loneliness and encourage her to express it. ___ ___ ___

I openly express my own feelings to my wife and tell her what I need. ___ ___ ___

I am learning to open up and overcome the tendencies to retreat into my shell. ___ ___ ___

Children

I let my wife and the children know that she is first in my affection. ___ ___ ___

I encourage a marriage-centered, not child-centered, home. ___ ___ ___

I give leadership to the spiritual training of our children through Bible reading and prayer. ___ ___ ___

Schedule

I am highly organized for each day, allowing no time for spontaneity and surprises. ___ ___ ___

I am a slave to the urgent request of outsiders, becoming a means to their ends. ___ ___ ___

My expectations of my
wife and children cause
them to feel pressured,
inadequate, unable to
please.

	Never	Occasionally	Frequently

Touching
I find ways each day to
touch and hold my wife
so she knows I
appreciate her.

I enjoy the delight of
caressing and hugging
without insisting it
culminate in sex
relations.

I keep myself inviting so
my wife is not repulsed
by offensive attitudes,
appearance, and odors.

Surprises
I think of special or
unusual things I could
do for or with my wife.

I arrange for surprise
events—eating out,
entertainment, trips,
weekends away.

I think of long-term
ways to stretch my
wife's interests and
opportunities for
growth.

Gifts

I give my wife one large gift on her birthday, anniversary, and Christmas and this satisfies her all year. ___ ___ ___

I give small gifts on many unexpected occasions because I think of her often. ___ ___ ___

I usually give utilitarian gifts rather than personal ones that say to my wife, "You are specially appreciated." ___ ___ ___

Shared Ideas

I have outgrown my wife and do not positively encourage her development. ___ ___ ___

I plan relaxing times together so we can share our dreams. ___ ___ ___

I discuss fully with my wife our plans for our marriage, our children, our future. ___ ___ ___

Laughter

I do everything I can to make our house a fun place to come home to. ___ ___ ___

	Never	Occasionally	Frequently

I encourage meal times to be special, happy times with a positive atmosphere of interaction. ____ ____ ____

I freely share jokes and funny stories on myself rather than on other family members. ____ ____ ____

Sexual Games
I flirt with my wife and enjoy and encourage this kind of romance and aliveness. ____ ____ ____

I take an active part in our sex life with genuine pleasure and abandon. ____ ____ ____

I am aggressive in loving my wife, seeking to delight her in every way possible and not using sex against her as a weapon, tool, or reward. ____ ____ ____

Loving Friend
I keep my wife's confidences and do not withhold from her any secrets that affect our marriage. ____ ____ ____

	Never	Occasionally	Frequently

I am loyal to my wife and support and praise her publicly.

I encourage her in the face of difficulties and defeat and stand by her faithfully.

Acceptance
I have fully accepted my wife with all her personal traits and idiosyncracies.

I have forgiven everything in her past and do not hold anything against her.

I enjoy my wife and feel free to open my heart to her.

Loved—Special
I have a growing desire for my wife's happiness and comfort.

I am committed to learning my wife's unique love language and practicing it.

I constantly tell my wife how special she is as a friend, partner, and lover.

Dreariness

	Never	Occasionally	Frequently
I nag about household chores and feel tied down and resentful.	_____	_____	_____
I resent my wife's taking time for recreation, hobbies, shopping, Bible study group.	_____	_____	_____
I tend to be a workaholic and feel guilty about planning special days or weekends for relaxing together.	_____	_____	_____

NOTES

1. Robert A. Harper, *Extramarital Relations* (New York: Hawthorn Books, 1967), pp. 385-391.
2. Morton Hunt, "Sexual Behavior in the 1970's" *Playboy* (Chicago: Playboy Press, 1974), n.p.
3. Louis Harris Poll, 1978-79.
4. Alexander Lowen and Robert J. Levin, "The Case Against Cheating in Marriage," *Redbook* (June 1969). Condensed in *Reader's Digest* (November 1969).
5. Galatians 6:7 (TJB).
6. Proverbs 11:2 (TLB).
7. John Drescher, *When Opposites Attract* (St. Meinrad, Indiana: Abbey Press, 1979), p. 49.
8. Ed Wheat, *Love Life* (Grand Rapids: Zondervan Publishers, 1980), p. 181.
9. Marabel Morgan, *Total Joy* (Old Tappan, New Jersey: Fleming H. Revell, 1976), pp. 74, 75.
10. Lou Beardsley and Toni Spry, *The Fulfilled Woman* (Eugene, Oregon: Harvest House, 1975), p. 29.
11. Proverbs 31; Song of Solomon.
12. 1 John 4:7 (TLB).
13. James 1:13 (TJB).
14. 1 Peter 5:8 (TLB).
15. Hebrews 4:15 (KJV).
16. David Stoop, *Self-Talk* (Old Tappan, New Jersey: Fleming H. Revell, 1982), p. 33.
17. Proverbs 5:3, 4 (TEV); 5:15, 16, 19 (TLB); 6:27-29, 32 (TLB).

18. E. Stanley Jones, *The Way to Power and Poise* (Nashville: Abingdon Press, 1949), p. 258.
19. Philippians 4:8 (TLB).
20. Russell Conwell, *Acres of Diamonds* (New York: Harper and Row, 1915).
21. Margaret Hess, *Moody Monthly* (March 1976), pp. 75, 76.
22. Peter Kreitler with Bill Bruns, *Affair Prevention* (New York: Macmillan Publishing Co., 1981), p. 15.
23. Willard and Marguerite Beecher, *Beyond Success and Failure* (New York: Julian Press, 1966), p. 108.

About the Author

J. ALLAN PETERSEN is a seasoned family counselor and president/founder of Family Concern, Inc. He is the author of *The Myth of the Greener Grass* and the general editor of *For Men Only, For Women Only,* and *The Marriage Affair.* He and his wife, Evelyn, live in Morrison, Colorado.

POCKET GUIDES
NEW FROM TYNDALE

■ *Getting Out of Debt* by Howard L. Dayton, Jr. At last, a no-nonsense approach to your money problems. Here's advice on creating a budget, cutting corners, making investments, and paying off loans. Features a list of money-saving tips.

■ *Increase Your Personality Power* by Tim La-Haye. Why do you get angry? Afraid? Worried? Discover your unique personality type, then use it to live more effectively—at home, on the job, and under pressure. An easy-to-use format includes personality tests to take on your own.

■ *The Perfect Way to Lose Weight* by Charles T. Kuntzleman and Daniel V. Runyon. Anyone can lose fat—and keep it off permanently. This tested program, developed by a leading physical fitness expert, shows how. Helpful charts and safety tips round out this practical fat-loss plan.

■ *Strange Cults in America* by Bob Larson. An easy-reading update of six well-known cults: the Unification Church, Scientology, The Way International, Rajneesh, Children of God, and Transcendental Meditation. Includes special features on how to identify a cult and talk to a cult member.

■ *Temper Your Child's Tantrums* by Dr. James Dobson. You don't need to feel frustrated as a parent. The celebrated author and "Focus on the Family" radio host wants to give you the keys to firm, but loving, discipline in your home. Follow his proven counsel and watch the difference in your children.